Adirondack Splendor

By Den Linnehan

Library Of Congress Cataloging - In - Publication Data
ISBN 0-9740280-0-2

Linnehan Press Published 2004
Printed by Monroe Litho

Linnehan, Den Adirondack Splendor

Front Cover: Gill Brook
Page 1: Meacham Lake
Back Cover: Meacham Lake, Piercefield Flow, Jay Covered Bridge, Meacham Lake outlet, Harrietstown, Barnum Pond, Indian Lake, Rainbow Waterfall, Phelps Mountain.

Jacket design, front and back cover photographs by Den Linnehan.
All photographs taken by Den Linnehan with the exception of Lake Jenny taken by Rob Maher.

Next Page:

Indian Head In Fog
- Rob and Carol Maher, Den and Elaine Linnehan, Linda and Jim Schultz.

The Canister On MacNaughton Mountain July 1988
- Sign in please. Until the year 2001, when an aspiring 46er climbed one of the official trailless peaks, they were required to locate the canister at the top and sign in. They would also record the names of the previous three parties and submit this information to the ADK 46er historian who would verify the climb. Here Den and Sherry Linnehan sign in on MacNaughton, not an official 46er mountain, but over 4,000 feet.

Avalanche Trail
- Stephanie Linnehan hikes to the end of Avalanche Lake along the rock strewn trail.

Rocky Peak Ridge Sept. 6, 1987
- Adirondack Forty-Sixer celebration on top of Rocky Peak Ridge on September 6, 1987.
(Only grape juice, since we still had to climb down before dark!) Den Linnehan, Rob and Carol Maher.

Dedication

To those that enhanced my hiking experience.

This book is dedicated to:
Elaine, Stephanie, and Sherry Linnehan
Rob and Carol Maher
Jim and Linda Schultz
for sharing the sheer joy of hiking over
1,000 miles of Adirondack wilderness.

Indian Head

MacNaughton Canister
Den and Sherry Linnehan

Avalanche Trail
Stephanie Linnehan

46er on Rocky Peak Ridge
Den Linnehan
Carol and Rob Maher

Contents

Foreword

Piercefield Flow mist rise.

Mist - slowly burning off a nearby pond.
Mist - caressing the mountain tops.
Sunrise on a darkened forest trail.

Mountains - dark and foreboding.
Mountains - green and lush.
Mountains - challenging but rewarding.
Mountains - preserved for all generations to enjoy.

Water - at the break of day.
Water - cascading through thick forest greenery.
Water - mirroring images of nature.
Water - through early morning mist.

There is a satisfaction of being one with nature. Of gathering strength from its strength. As I paddle gently over the mountain reflective waters before dawn, all these visions return to me, still vivid after twenty five years of photographing the Adirondacks.

During this adventure I acquired a deep love of nature, well beyond my initial feelings. On one of those early morning days drifting toward sunrise I starting photographing the Adirondacks. I have selected a few images that bring back that mood and the memory. More than one third of the photographs were taken within one hundred feet of a road, another third only after a 10+ mile hike, and the final third somewhere in between. I love the early morning and twilight thus many of my photographs are of recognizable Adirondack areas either before dawn or just after, usually "scouted" the day before. In some areas, I have photographed the same scene in all four seasons. Come with me to explore these moods and memories in Adirondack Splendor.

New York's North country is synonymous with the Adirondack Forest Preserve protected by state law to remain "forever wild". It comprises approximately 6 million acres, about the size of the state of Vermont. The Adirondack State Park has over 2,000 miles of trails. Within the park are 2,300 lakes and ponds with more than 1,000 miles of rivers fed by an estimated 30,000 miles of brooks and streams.

On September 6, 1987 I, along with Carol and Rob Maher became Forty-Sixers, one who has climbed all 46 Adirondack Mountains over 4000 feet. We hiked many of the high peaks together although I did over ten 4000 foot mountains alone. Jim Schultz hiked many of the trailed peaks with us. All hikes were one day trips. This meant sometimes starting out at 3 AM and finishing beyond 9 PM on an 18 mile trailless hike. We would often drive up on a Friday, hike Saturday and drive the 6 hours back to Rochester, New York Sunday night, just to spend a few more hours within the Adirondack Preserve.

Adirondack Loj road sunrise.

As a newly married couple in the 1970's, Elaine and I camped at Fish Creek and Rollins Pond, Indian Lake, the Lake George battlefield, and the Adirondack Loj lean-tos. As our two daughters (Stephanie and Sherry) grew up, we began to rent cabins and cottages on Lake Flower, Upper Saranac Lake, the Ray Brook area and Lake Placid. This book is dedicated to my family who waited patiently as I took just one more Adirondack picture, sometimes an hour or so later. Well, maybe 2 or 3 hours later! We would spend at least 2 days each trip canoeing, usually on Upper or Lower Saranac Lake stopping at its many islands to picnic, swim, or relax.

I utilized a Nikon camera with 35 mm, 50 mm and a 85 mm to 210 mm zoom lenses. In many low light situations, especially the waterfalls and fireworks scenes, a tripod was necessary. I used Kodachrome 64 and Ektachrome 64 slide film and Kodak print film.

Gill Brook late morning.

I was fortunate to work for Eastman Kodak for 32+ years and gave travel log shows to Kodak audiences of around 1500 people on 4 separate occasions. The shows were National Parks, Central Europe, New York State, and my latest show called "Adirondack Splendor". It consisted of 6 projectors with over 1,000 slides. I took one year to write the script, select the slides, and assemble this production. This book is the culmination of my travel log "Adirondack Splendor". I hope these photographs inspire you to visit and come to know the Adirondacks with the same awe and reverence that I now possess.

Lake Placid Region

Mirror Lake

Samuel de Champlain was probably the first white man to discover the Adirondacks in 1609. A 1776 map of the Adirondacks showed this land was not surveyed. Not until 1779, almost one hundred and seventy years after Champlain's discovery, did anyone show much interest in these mountains. Alexander Macomb purchased 4 million acres at 8 pence an acre. By 1880 hotels were built in the Adirondacks thus making the region a popular resort. About 125,000 people live in more than one hundred towns, villages, and hamlets within the Adirondack preserve. A late evening reflection on Mirror Lake in the town of Lake Placid.

Mirror Lake

- A time exposure before sunrise. One of the most popular destinations is the town of Lake Placid. World class sporting competitions include ice hockey, ice skating, bobsled and luge in the winter. In the summer golf, tennis, hiking, and canoeing. In the autumn spectacular fall foliage.

Lake Placid

- A panoramic view along Route 86, near the Lake Placid golf course, just before sunset.

Views of Pitchoff Mountain, Cascade Mountain, Hopkins and Green Mountains, Giant Mountain, Mount Van Hoevenberg, Round, Noonmark, The Range, and the ski jump towers.

Riverside Drive

- Sentinel Range Wilderness area early morning. This range consists of three major mountain peaks: Stewart, Kilburn, and Sentinel. Hiking is limited since there are very few views from the top of these three peaks. Many blowdowns exist. There are two trails, the North and South Notch trails that start on the River Road.

Lake Placid Horse Show

- Off of Route 73 in view of the North and South Notch Mountains, every July 4th, the "I Love New York State" horse show is held. Competition is spread out over a two week time frame and varies from amateur to professional.

Mount Josephine

- Mist rising off of Mount Josephine on a cold fall day.

Adirondack Loj Area

- In the 1920's hiking trails, campsites, and many lean-tos were developed. Over 2,000 miles of foot trails are now maintained throughout the park. Fall colors on Colden, Wright, Algonguin, Iroquois, Boundary, Wallface, Street and Nye mountain with Mount Jo in the foreground.

Adirondack Loj Road

- Strong winds in late September shape clouds into mesmerizing patterns.

Adirondack Loj Road

Luge Run

- Dermot Organ sledding for USA luge and Miro Zayonc sledding for Team Canada rehearse the luge course mentally before their run.

Bob Sled Run

- A two man team prepares for the critical start of the Bob Sled run on Mount Van Hoevenberg.

Mount Van Hoevenberg

- One travels down the Adirondack Loj road and turns onto the South Meadow Road for the beginning of this trail. The first mile does little climbing. One more mile of easy climbing to the top of Mount Van Hoevenberg with these views. From left to right: Algonquin range, Wallface Mountain, Street, Nye, and Mt. Jo in the foreground. If one continues over the mountain one would see the Olympic bobsled and luge runs.

Mount Whitney

- When Colvin came to the Adirondacks in the 1870's he called for the mountains protection, while beginning topographical surveys of this land. His cherished land 100 years later as seen from Mount Whitney surrounded in fog, overlooks Lake Placid and the High Peaks region. Governor Hill signed Colvin's forever wild proposal into law on May 15,1885. Section 8 states this forest preserve shall be forever kept as wild forest land.

Views From Mount Whitney

- Mount Whitney is a trailless peak under 2000 feet. Your hike should take about twenty minutes with spectacular views of the High Peaks to the south and Lake Placid to the west. This morning Lake Placid was draped in mist and we decided to admire the scenery. Over three hours were spent watching as the mountains appeared through the mist. It seems we spent the entire day admiring the views now towards sunset.

Saranac Lake Region

Bluff Island

The Saranac region: one rich in history, great estates, beautiful lakes, and mountain scenery. The Indians called Lower Saranac Lake " lake of the clustered stars". If you get a chance, take a canoe out at midnight on a summer night, and you'll agree --- the name was aptly chosen. We'll rent our canoes at Crescent Bay. After carefully packing our camping gear, food, clothing, and camera, we'll paddle and stop at numerous islands for a long swim. Some barely support a small tree --- others are 6 acres or more in size. Bluff Island on Lower Saranac Lake is a favorite spot to canoe and have a picnic lunch.

Lake Flower

- Canoeing at sunrise and sunset is serene. It produced a myriad of beautiful shades of purple and yellow. McKenzie Mountain to the east with Scarface Mountain to the south.

Saranac Lake

- Sunset on
Lower Saranac Lake.

Lake Flower

- Lake Flower reflecting
McKenzie Mountain.

Lake Colby

- Mist rising on Lake Colby in the town of Saranac Lake.

Simon Pond

- State Bridge area. The fog burned off the lake in less than thirty minutes on a cold twenty degree October morning.

Baker Mountain

- Probably the best view for the shortest climb in all the Adirondacks. Baker mountain overlooks the town of Saranac Lake, the High Peaks, McKenzie Pond and Flower Lake.

Baker Mountain

- It was 7 below zero in Saranac Lake on New Year's Day when we made this climb up Baker Mountain.

An Adirondack Great Camp

- Sagamore was built by William West Durant in 1897 on a 300 acre site as a year round residence. He constructed many other great camps including Camp Pine Knot and Camp Uncas. The Sagamore main lodge is a 3 1/2 story building with the first floor 76 by 104 feet. The camp contains 29 buildings. Tours are available.

Camp Sagamore

- The great camp was all log construction, a combination of early log cabin and Swiss chalet. Sagamore logs were cut from the surrounding site. The entire structure was given a rustic appearance by sheets of peeled cedar bark applied over the frame construction. The inside has polished beams with ceilings and walls of birch treated with bees wax.

County Route 45 area

- Early morning near Coreys and the Cold River Ranch just before the frost melted.

County Route 45 area

Miller Brook South Creek

- Approaching Middle Saranac Lake just off Route 3 is Miller Brook. On the south side of the road is a fishing access site. On the north side one could paddle to Middle Saranac Lake.

Fish Creek
And Rollins Pond

- We camped many times at Fish Creek and Rollins Pond State campgrounds. Of the 45 campgrounds within the Adirondack Park Fish Creek Pond campground is my favorite. Over 350 excellent camp sites are available throughout the summer and fall months. Many nature hikes start within the park. One can hike the Floodwood loop and Otter Hollow loop. Rollins Pond was opened in 1955 and has over 280 campsites. You can rent rowboats, canoes, kayaks, or paddle boats. Fishing is popular at Rollins Pond. Yellow perch, brown bullhead, northern pike, and bass fill the placid waters.

Floodwood Mountain

- A short easy hike of a around three and one half miles round trip. Just past the town of Saranac Inn is Floodwood Road. Travel this gravel and dirt road for 7 long miles. One will pass near Hoel Pond and pass Floodwood Pond where camping is permissible. At the end of the road is a Boy Scout Reservation. The trail leads through a field and starts to climb through a hardwood forest. The final 1/2 mile is steep. Views from sunrise past sunset.

Floodwood Mountain

- Be prepared if traversing this after dark. Two very steep sections are at the top which require care and at least a flashlight for the initial steep descent down an otherwise easy trail.

Lake Flower

- Each July 4th celebration at Flower Lake culminates with spectacular fireworks. Given a good tripod, many time exposures usually at f16 or greater, 3 to 5 seconds of time, a 35 mm lens, a piece of cardboard to cover the lens between bursts, and a little luck correctly pointing the camera, the results can be spectacular.

Marcy Dam Region

Algonquin / Boundary Mountain

To the southwest of Wright is the highest peak in this range and the second tallest in the Adirondacks: Algonquin. It is 5114 feet, spectacular in July or October. Algonquin was first climbed on August 8, 1837 by Ebenezer Emmons. South west of Algonquin stands Boundary Peak so named because it denoted the ancient boundary between the Algonquin and Iroquois Indians. Continuing west is Iroquois Peak at 4840 feet. Cairns lead the way from Algonquin to Boundary and Iroquois. Note Whiteface Mountain, partially blocked by the large boulder, in the distance.

Marcy Dam

- In 1906 the forever wild constitution was amended so that 3% of the forest preserve could be flooded to store water. It passed in 1912 and 1913. This area, Marcy Dam, was the site of a lumber mill, used for guiding logs down Marcy Brook. In 1915 the lumber companies wanted to cut all remaining mature timber but that amendment was rejected by the voters. Two easy trails lead to Marcy Dam. One from Heart Lake is 2.3 miles each way. The other option is the South Meadow trail. It is 2.6 miles long and relatively flat.

View From Mount Josephine

- Mount Jo was named by Henry Van Hoevenberg in honor of his finance, Josephine Schofield. A 700 foot elevation increase gives these views. Heart Lake directly below. In the distance is Colden, Wright, Algonquin, Iroquois, with Indian Pass far right. This hike of one mile each way is a great way to experience the Adirondacks with minimal effort.

Mount Josephine

- Surrounding us on a winter climb of Mount Jo are ice formations, and plenty of snow. In December a much tougher climb, but still relatively easy if dressed properly. Two routes lead to the top. The shorter route does have one steep section, so for new hikers I would choose the longer trail, especially in winter.

Phelps Mountain

- On this early fall day we note that winter has arrived.

Trailless Donaldson Mountain

- We decided to climb 3 trailless peaks in July traversing the same mountains twice in order to get out, about 20 miles total: Seward, Donaldson, and Emmons. On the return to Donaldson mountain our day turned from bright sun to threatening clouds and then hail, with 4 hours of heavy rain drenching us with 8 miles of herd path still to negotiate. It was barely above freezing. Ampersand Lake and Mountain are directly below.

Phelps Mountain

- A moderate 4 mile hike from Marcy Dam area even in early October. Phelps was first climbed in 1904 by Charles Wood. Colvin named this for Old Man Phelps, a colorful philosopher and long time guide in the Adirondacks. From Phelps views across the valley of snow covered Wright and Algonquin mountains.

Marshall Mountain

- Rob and Carol Maher climb the slide to trailless Marshall.

Street And Nye Mountain

- Rob and Carol Maher winding through small trees up trailless Street and Nye.

Gray Mountain

- Rob Maher on a decaying corduroy towards Gray.

Trailless Hiking

- Twenty of the forty six mountains above 4000 feet in the Adirondacks are "trailless". Trails in the Adirondacks vary greatly from well worn trails with signs, to herd paths, to total bushwhacking. Hikers may start their adventure through dense forests crossing many roaring streams, especially in the spring. Most trailless hikes now have some sort of herd path to follow, but none of these are marked trails. Careful planning is needed to successfully climb these peaks. One should feel comfortable in map reading and compass use in a forest environment. Many trailless start on marked trails and lead up a wash, a dried up stream, or climb up a slide, or go straight through a pine forest. As one continues deeper into the forest you will walk through the Adirondack black mud, negotiate around bogs, marshes, and swamps, or slowly make your way through a recent blow down.

Esther, Macomb, Allen, Marshall, Seward

Emmons, Seymour, Couchsachraga, Hough, Santanoni

South Dix, Street, Gray Peak, Panther, Tabletop

Donaldson, East Dix, Cliff, Redfield, Nye

Trailless Canisters

- Hiking the trailless peaks started in 1924 with Robert and George Marshall defining the 46 peaks over 4000, 20 of which had no trails. Hikers organized a climbing group known as the Adirondack Forty Sixers. All 20 canisters photographed on our 46er quest. In the past one would record the names of the three people who climbed the mountain before you and send the information to the historian as proof of the climb. All canisters have now been removed to preserve the Adirondack wilderness.

Algonquin Peak

- To the southwest of Wright is the highest peak in this range and the second tallest in the Adirondacks. Algonquin is 5114 feet, spectacular in July. Algonquin was first climbed on August 8, 1837 by Ebenezer Emmons. A strenuous hike of 4 miles each way from the Adirondack Loj's High Peaks Information Center. The ascent of nearly 3000 feet within 4 miles makes it one of the toughest in the Adirondacks.

Wright Mountain

- The MacIntyre range rises southwest of Heart Lake, having been named for the dominate figure of the iron-works, Archibald McIntyre. Wright Mountain was named for a New York Governor, Silas Wright.

Avalanche Lake

- A round trip of 10 miles leads to one of the most spectacular boulder strewn trail in the Adirondacks. Probably Indian Pass trail would be a close second. Looking east at Avalanche Lake is Mount Colden, on the right, and Avalanche Mountain, on the left. On this rugged trail one must negotiate two wooden planks bolted into the rock at "Hitch-up Matildas" pass and squeeze through and around huge boulders. The sheer rock walls rise directly out of the water of Avalanche Lake. Allow plenty of time to enjoy the massive slides on Colden. At the end of the lake are trails to Mount Colden and Lake Colden.

Heart Lake

- One of the easiest areas to reach within the High Peaks is Heart Lake. About five miles of paved road lead to the Adirondack Loj lodge and the Adirondack Mountain Club parking lot. After paying the entrance fee, one can hike about 5 minutes to reach Heart Lake.

Rocky Falls

Rocky Falls

- A relatively flat walk of about five miles, round trip, brings you to this secluded waterfall. The trail passes Heart Lake, enters a mature forest, and crosses a few small streams until a side trail leads to Rocky Falls and a lean-to. In the summertime a good swimming spot.

Indian Pass

- Hiking towards Indian Pass one is immersed in an immense one mile long gorge. A stream is passed near the edge of Scott Clearing Lean-to at 3.8 miles. Huge boulders 20 feet across or more lay near the trail, making this a difficult hike. I took the high water route, although it has some steep climbing. At 5.0 miles the trail ascends into the pass with some very difficult hiking. At 5.5 miles one begins to see views of the cliffs in Indian Pass, almost 1000 feet high.

Summit Rock

- On a perfect fall day at 10 AM is Wallface Mountain. Spectacular colorful views of the huge boulders in the gorge below to the sheer cliffs on the foothold of Wallface.

Wallface Mountain

- Towards noon the sun emerged from behind a few stubborn mist like clouds and shown brightly for at least one hour revealing the stunning beauty of the 1000 foot Wallface cliff. One can see hundreds of full grown trees within the sheltered crevasses. This view is from Summit Rock utilizing a telescopic lens.

Wanika Waterfall Area

- A round trip of 13 plus miles of fairly flat and soggy trail leads to these beautiful waterfalls. One starts this hike on the Northville Lake Placid trail just outside of the town of Lake Placid.

Wanika Waterfall

- The trail follows the Chubb River, then crosses a large spruce swamp, merges onto many old tote roads, and finally reaches a lean-to about 100 yards from the falls. The upper portion of Wanika Waterfall, around 25 feet high.

Cascade Region

Cascade Waterfall

After three inches of rain the night before, I make my way up a herd path to Cascade Waterfall.

Pitchoff Mountain

- This mountain is a series of steep climbs up bare rocks to various lookouts. Here giant boulders force us to reconsider our path. This bare ridge, at 3600 feet, offers excellent views to the west and south. We traversed all 5 peaks covering a trail of over 6 miles one way. Many rock formations and fascinating boulders are seen along the trailed, although sometimes hard to follow route.

Lower Cascade Lake

- Cascade Mountain on the left. Pitchoff Mountain foothills on the right.

Owls Head Mountain

- For a round trip hike of less than two miles, this rocky small peak offers great views. Smaller mountains like Spread Eagle, Blueberry, Hedgehog, Hopkins, Rooster Comb, and Snow can be seen in the distance. Many 4000 foot mountains are also visible: Cascade, Pitchoff, Giant.

Cascade Mountain

- A favorite hike of many starting out to experience the Adirondack high peaks. It is an easy 2.4 mile hike one way. The ascent is less than 2000 feet for a 4098 foot mountain. Cascade Mountain is named for the cascade of water that flows between the two Cascade Lakes. Fog streamed through the forest on one of our three hikes we made up this mountain.

Jay Region

Jay Covered Bridge

Roads opened the Adirondacks along with covered bridges. Twenty one exist in New York State. This was the only remaining one in the Adirondack region at Jay New York. Jay Covered Bridge crosses the east branch of the Ausable River. It was built in 1857 and is 175 feet long. It has been taken down for repairs and will be rebuilt over the same spot as a pedestrian bridge.

Jay Covered Bridge

- The rugged Jay Range of mountains form a picturesque backdrop for the Jay Covered Bridge. Normally this makes a great place to slide down a few rocks and have the water gently coax you along. This was July 5, 1997. Stephanie Linnehan, our daughter, watches the raging water after 3 inches of rain the day before.

Whiteface Region

Whiteface Mountain

About eight thousand years ago repeating melting and freezing of a valley glacier caused the rocks to break off creating the rugged head wall of Whiteface. It is the 5th highest Adirondack mountain. Due to its total 4867 elevation, Whiteface is a major ski center and one of the largest in the east having a vertical drop of over 3000 feet.

Owens, Copperas, and Winch Pond Trail

- For less than 3 miles of hiking with little climbing, Owens, Copperas, and Winch Pond trails are a popular destination. One can picnic, swim, and camp at the lean-to on Copperas Pond. There are excellent views of Whiteface Mountain to the north.

West Branch Of The Ausable River

- The Ausable River rages between flume like rock walls in the Flume Falls and High Falls Gorge. For a fee, you can traverse High Falls Gorge through a series of narrow walkways built into the rock ledges.

Esther Mountain

- The northern most of the Adirondack High Peaks was named for Esther Macomb. In 1839 she tried to climb Whiteface from the north, became lost and climbed Esther instead.

The Flume Falls

- On Route 86 just past the Whiteface ski center, the Ausable River passes under a metal bridge and through a series of rock cliffs and large boulders. Whiteface and Esther Mountain are in the background.

Catamount Mountain

- Less than 4 miles round trip with an ascent of 1542 feet, Catamount's south side bare rock summit makes this visit worth the effort. Even more exciting, near the top one must traverse through a very steep chimney in the rocks.

Catamount Mountain

- Lichens growing on the rocks at the top of Catamount Mountain.

Connery Pond

- Less than a one mile hike to Connery Pond. One year I hiked it five times to obtain these views. Fall colors prevail one day. Fog the next and snow on my last visit.

Silver Lake Preserve
(Next Page)

- An easy hike over wood boards through the heart of a bog. Many benches are placed throughout the hike of 30 minutes. A longer and steeper hike of an additional 15 minutes takes you to a bluff overlooking Silver Lake.

SILVER LAKE PRESERVE
This Preserve is a gift of
BETTY HICKS
GREENLEAF CHASE
EDWIN KETCHLEDGE
THE HAWKEYE CONSERVATIONISTS
NANCY M. KIMBALL
WARD LUMBER CO.

Keene And Keene Valley Region

Keene Area

The Range trail consists of two parts: The ADK Range trail leads from Johns Brook over Upper Wolf Jaw, Armstrong, Gothics with a side trail to Lower Wolf Jaw. The State Range trail traverses Saddleback, Basin and connects to Haystack and then Mount Marcy trails. It is a very rugged but spectacular trail. The Range consists of a series of mountains over 4000 feet stretching for over 7 miles with a total ascent of near 5000 feet. Farm land one mile south of Keene at the Route 73 9N junction.

Pyramid Mountain

- Although not a 46er mountain, Pyramid is over 4000 feet high. Located between Sawteeth and Gothics, it offers one of the most spectacular views in the Adirondacks. Jim Schultz views Gothics, Saddleback, Basin, and Haystack Mountains in the foreground. In the distance is Wright, Algonquin, Boundary and Iroquois, Marshall, and Marcy.

Hopkins Mountain area

Hopkins Mountain

- An elevation increase of over 2100 feet makes this 6.4 mile round trip mountain a challenge although there are no really steep inclines to negotiate. After 3/4 of a mile one sees a side trail to Mossy Cascade. Twenty-two major peaks over 4000 feet can be seen from the top. In the distance: Dix, Nipple Top, Colvin, Sawteeth, Pyramid, Gothics, Armstrong, Upper and Lower Wolf Jaw. In the foreground: Round, Noonmark, Bear Den, Snow and Rooster Comb and Hedgehog.

Blueberry Mountain

- A beautiful climb with the first mile through woods and rushing streams. After making a sharp turn at this huge boulder, the trail becomes very steep and strewn with rocks. It is 2.4 miles each way.

Blueberry Mountain

- Porter and Cascade Mountain can be seen from the top where one huge boulder remains from the ice age.

Snow Mountain

- At 2360 feet, Snow offers fine views of the surrounding higher peaks. We took the Adirondack Trail Improvement Society trail to Snow and Rooster Comb.

Big Slide Mountain

- Utilizing the Phelps Trail over the Three Brothers Mountains for about 2.4 miles one comes to this slide which occurred in the 1830s and from which the mountain takes its name.

Cliff Mountain

- Very few views for a very steep ascent on this trailless mountain. This unusual halo around the sun was the only bright spot on a rather dismal mountain.

Lake Jenny Bridge

- This wooden bridge crosses Lake Jenny towards Allen Mountain.

Haystack Mountain

- The view from near the top of Haystack Mountain, 4960 feet, the third highest in the Adirondacks. Wright, Algonquin, Boundary and Iroquois in the background. Colvin said Haystack was the "Matterhorn of the Adirondacks". In the foreground is the Range Trail and Basin mountain. Twenty seven major high peaks are discernible from Haystack. The Haystack Trail is one of the steepest climbs in the Adirondacks gaining 1100 feet in only eight tenths of a mile.

Saddleback Mountain

- Completing The Range from the Keene Valley, we pass a large recent rock slide, and continue up Ore Bed Brook to Saddleback. In my opinion, probably the 2nd steepest descent in all the Adirondacks and the most dangerous.

Mount Marcy

- The tallest mountain in New York State at 5344 feet. Enshrouded in mist is Skylight Mountain. It was named in 1837 to honor Governor William Marcy.

Lichens

- On the ground you will see hundreds of colorful odd looking growths which look more like cracked paint that plants. These primitive plants are lichens and they grow where there is no soil by breaking down the rock chemically to create a fine layer of soil so other low shrubs can survive.

Rock Formations

- Smooth and polished rock formations weave a mosaic pattern in sand filled depressions.

- A coarse rock juts out abruptly in a pine forest high above the raging waters below.

Lily

Monarch Butterfly on a Zinnia

Water Lily

Milkweed

Lichens

Saint Huberts Region

Adirondack Mountain Reserve Lake Road

Saint Huberts area has over 90 miles of spectacular hiking trails with most starting on private land owned by the Adirondack Mountain Reserve. The Saint Huberts region was named for the patron saint of hunted deer. As the story goes, Hubert was hunting on Good Friday and a stag with a crucifix between his antlers reprimanded him for hunting. He was so shaken that he became a protector of animals. When the Adirondack Mountain Club purchased thousands of acres in 1890 they named their clubhouse "Saint Hubert Inn". The road gains around 700 feet in elevation over the 3 1/2 mile traverse. Many trails branch off of this main road to climb 4000 foot peaks. Shorter trails exist with views of waterfalls, rivers, and forest.

West River Trail

- This trail is over 8 miles of forest walking with very little climbing. Seen here are Colvin and Sawteeth Mountains across Beaver Meadows. This path follows the Ausable River for many miles through beautiful forests.

The Adirondack Mountain Reserve / Ausable Club

- A private group owning and preserving over 10 miles of Adirondack wilderness. Over 90 miles of trails are within this area. All land over 4000 feet in elevation was purchased by the Adirondack Park Agency on top of Noonmark in 1978. The state also obtained permanent public easements for foot travel on the Adirondack Mountain Reserve hiking trails with the exception of some trails around Upper Ausable Lake.

Noonmark And Giant

- A few miles south of Keene Valley is Saint Huberts. These views are from the road near the Adirondack Mountain Reserve Club. Noonmark Mountain is a short hike of 2 miles with views in all directions. Giant Mountain is a medium hike of 3 miles but ascent of over 3000 feet.

Mount Colvin

- Careful planning is needed for a one day round trip to Upper Ausable Lake and back. One must ascend over 5200 feet in elevation and hike over 18 miles from the Lake Road starting point. I started my climb in total darkness walking the Lake Road before dawn on a crisp fall morning. I arrived at Mount Colvin around 9 AM. I then headed towards Blake Mountain and descend a steep trail, down 2100 feet in 1.9 miles, to the Upper Ausable Lake area. It is now 10 am. One mile in 15 minutes on the Carry Trail.

Sawteeth Mountain

- After spending an enjoyable hour and a half talking to the workers at Upper Ausable Lake, I start up Sawteeth. It is now 11:45 AM. I am only half way! I have 2.8 miles and a 2100 foot ascent of Sawteeth, then a 3.0 mile 2300 foot descent of Sawteeth. I make it to the top of Sawteeth by 2:30 PM. Just one more picture and I head down Sawteeth just before dusk. A tough 18 mile hike. Seen here is Sawteeth mountain on the main road to the club house. The Adirondack Mountain Reserve golf course is open to the public on selected days.

Fish Hawk Cliffs

- A hike of less than two tenths of a mile from Indian Head leads to Fish Hawk Cliffs. Legend says as the chieftain passed away, a thunder bolt hit this rock and engraved his likeness in the cliff above, hence the name Indian Head.

Indian Head Views

- Indian Head rises 750 feet directly above Lower and Upper Ausable Lakes. Mt. Colvin to the south and Sawteeth Mountain to the north silhouetted in shadows.

Indian Head Trail

- After hiking the Lake Road for 3 1/2 miles one approaches Lower Ausable Lake. Indian Head Trail starts to climb a series of switchbacks to a view of Gothics called the "Gothics Window" at three tenths of a mile. The trail climbs a ladder, passes a mossy cliff, and then climbs steeply to the bare ledges where spectacular views are present in all directions.

Round Mountain

- The summit of Round Mountain has views in all directions. One can make a loop hike of less than five miles. As one approaches the open rocks on Round Mountain the last 500 feet are marked with cairns that must be carefully followed. That day I had the entire mountain to myself. Views of Noonmark and The Range to the west. To the east views of the cliffs on Giant and Rocky Peak Ridge.

Round Pond And Trail

- A half mile hike, just off of Route 73, leads to Round Pond. The trail begins very steeply traversing the side hill, levels out, and then drops down to Round Pond. This trail ultimately leads to Dix Mountain still another 6 1/2 miles of strenuous climbing up 3200 feet to the top of Dix.

Bald Peak To Rocky Peak Ridge And Giant

- One of the most spectacular hikes in the Adirondacks with over 5 miles of open hiking along numerous rock ledges. It is extremely strenuous with a total ascent of over 5300 feet. The hike is 11 miles one way. You will need to bring two cars and park one at each end of the trail.

Bald Peak

Rocky Peak Ridge

- Along the route one climbs over Blueberry Cobbles at 2.0 miles and Bald Peak (3060) at 3.9 miles. After climbing through the Dickerson Notch we ascend Rocky Peak Ridge (4060) seen here and then Giant (4420). Finally a 3 mile hike down to the road.

Giant Mountain

Giant Mountain Ledge

- Starting on the Ridge Trail to Giant this trail utilizes many switchbacks to climb to an open ledge at seven tenths of a mile. From these ledges on Giant Mountain at sunrise, one can view Chapel Pond, Round Mountain, and in the distance The Range.

From Giant Mountain Ledges

- Mist was caressing the hilltops as I climbed up part of Giant Mountain to view the Chapel Pond cliffs across the valley. In the top photo you can see the valley between the huge cliffs that I climbed. I started near the pond's south corner hugging the cliffs and continued up where you see bare rock.

From Chapel Pond Cliffs

- A view straight down to Chapel Pond and across to the shoulder of Giant Mountain.

Chapel Pond Cliffs

- I decided one day to climb up the cliffs on Chapel Pond. No ropes, just hiking as far up the mountain as possible climbing over huge boulders that had fallen into the crevasse. I assumed I could eventually reach the top, but to my chagrin, the stone walls kept rising the more I climbed. After climbing for more than 45 minutes, I eventually ended up in a dead end canyon high above the valley surrounded by cliffs on three sides. Coming back down was very difficult and very slow.

Overlook South of Giant

- A panoramic view of Chapel Pond, a ridge on Giant and the huge cliffs south of Chapel Pond. This unmarked trail leads to a huge cliff only 200 feet off the road. If one traverses around the cliff to the south and then climbs up a steep bank to the north you will be at the top of this lookout in about 10 minutes.

Chapel Pond Area

- Huge boulders, 7 to 9 feet high, rest near the base of Chapel Pond. It is a fascinating area to explore.

Chapel Pond

- Our starting point for the first hike up Giant was Chapel Pond at 1628 feet elevation.

Indian Head - Colvin and Sawteeth Mountain

- Verplanck Colvin was the Superintendent of State Land Survey starting in 1872. He surveyed the Adirondack region for almost 30 years. He was largely responsible for the inauguration of the Adirondack Park and State Forest Preserve which he urged in 1868. Climbing is steady up Colvin, seen here on the left, with several steep pitches near the top. It is a relatively steep ascent of 2300 feet for a 4068 foot mountain traversing 2.9 miles one way from the lake. Another 8 miles is added for walking the private road.

Gothics, Armstrong, Upper And Lower Wolf Jaw Mountains

- Sawteeth, prior page, at 4134 feet is a difficult 3.0 mile climb along the saw teeth like peaks. Outlooks at 250 and 800 feet and a precipitous view of Lower Ausable Lake thirteen hundred feet below are alone worth the climb. From Indian Head left to right: Mount Colvin, Upper Ausable Lake, Sawteeth, Pyramid, Gothics, Armstrong, Upper and Lower Wolf Jaw Mountains with Lower Ausable Lake below.

Rainbow Waterfall

- Views in summer and fall (next page). After hiking down the Lake Road for 3 1/2 miles, this path skirts the Lower Ausable Lake and continues for about one tenth of a mile climbing over some large boulders. Huge cliffs beckon you onward deeper into this chasm. Bob Ellis views the 150 foot Rainbow Waterfall.

Rainbow Waterfall

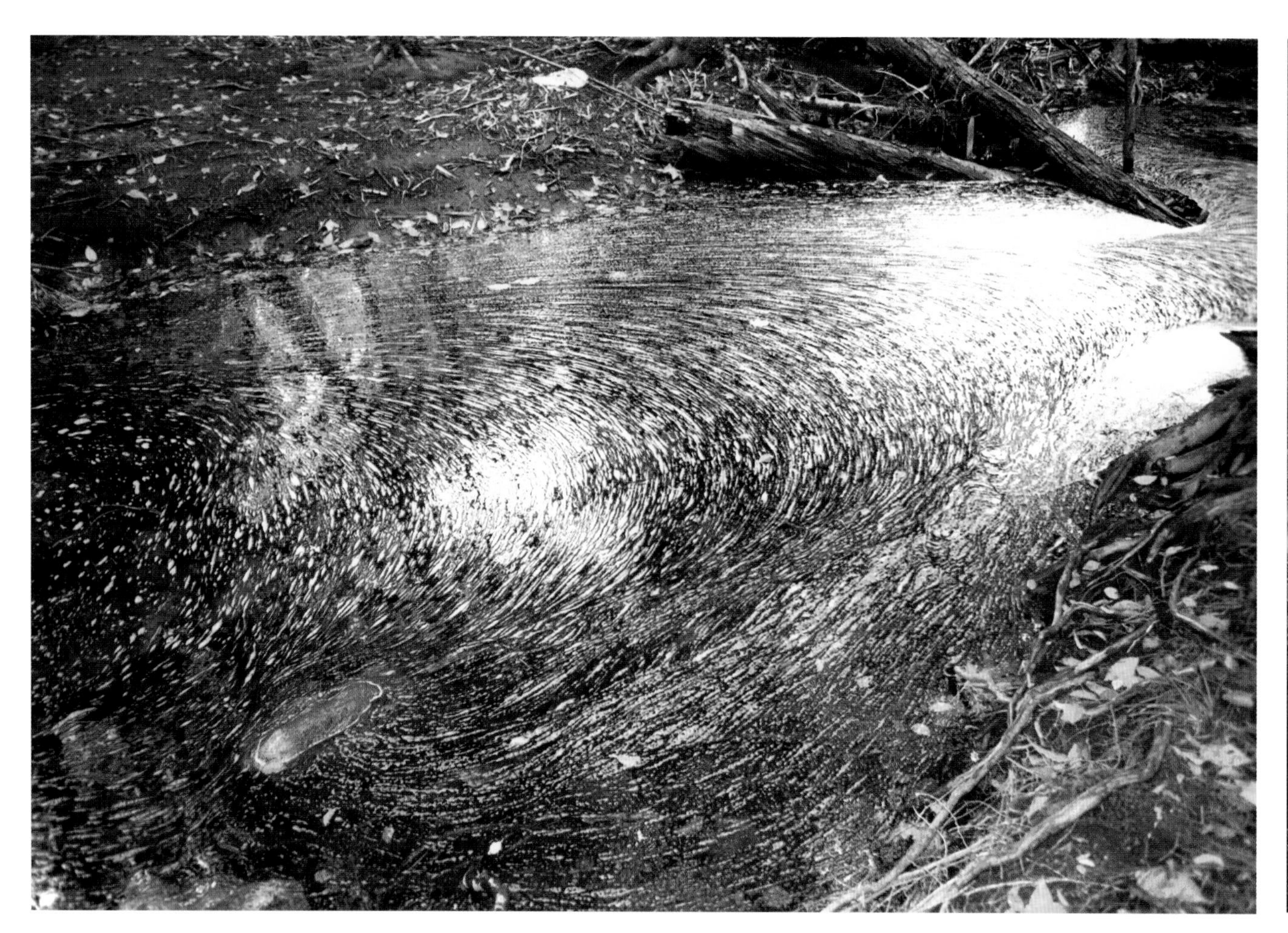

Adirondack Mountain Reserve

- Near the dam area on the Lake Road, the Ausable River meanders through a boulder filled stream for almost another mile before it leaves the Adirondack Mountain Reserve.

Gill Brook

Gill Brook

- Following the private Lake Road from the Ausable Club, around the locked gate, one travels only a mile or so to reach ten beautiful small waterfalls tucked away among the boulders.

Gill Brook

Adirondack Mountain Reserve

Gill Brook

- Another spectacular waterfall along the river section.

Beaver Meadow Falls

- Along the West River trail, Bear Run, Cathedral Rocks, Pyramid Brook, and Wedge Brook. Beaver Meadow Falls is reached at 2.7 miles. These falls have almost a bridal veil appearance and are beautiful in late summer and early fall.

Mossy Cascade Waterfall

Mossy Cascade Waterfall

- On the trail to Hopkins mountain, a 600 foot side trip over rough and slippery terrain leads to this waterfall tucked into a glen. It is less than a one mile hike from the road to the junction of this side trail.

Elk Pass

- On a trip to climb Bear Den, Dial, and Nipple Top mountains,
we stop briefly to capture the colors within this small swamp.

Split Rock Falls

- Near the town of New Russia the Boquet River creates this fascinating waterfall and swimming area.

Elk Lake And Newcomb Region

Clear Pond

A dirt road leads 5 miles to the Elk Lake Lodge. Most of the trails here start on private land. They are very rugged trails and require extra care and planning to complete if climbing as a day hike. We started our day climb of four trailless peaks (Macomb, South Dix, East Dix, and Hough Peak) at 3 AM. Our day ended at 9 PM. Fifteen miles of hiking and 4000 feet increase in elevation. For most of the trailless peaks, we made it more interesting by missing the slide on Macomb (about 100 feet below us) and wandered upward through thick pine trees finding a slide about 1/2 mile from the summit.

Elk Lake

-You can rent cottages including meals at Elk Lake Lodge for this spectacular early morning view of Elk Lake and the High Peaks.

High Peaks Surrounding Elk Lake And Sunrise Mountain

-Towards the west is Allen Mountain with the North River Mountains in the far distance. To the east is Macomb and the Dix Mountain Wilderness. This view is from Sunrise Mountain.

Newcomb Visitor Interpretive Center

- Within a day one can climb Goodnow Mountain and tour the Visitor Interpretive Center. Three trails, of less than a mile each, exist and range from easy to moderate. Rich Lake Trail has views of Goodnow Mountain and the fire tower. These trees are on the Sucker Brook Trail which has wetlands and mixed hardwoods. On the Peninsula Trail one finds hemlock trees over 200 years old. This trail skirts the rocky peninsula of Rich Lake. Many boardwalks and wooden stairs make this trail very easy.

Goodnow Mountain And Fire Tower

- Sylvester Goodnow lived at the base of this mountain that now bears his name. A few miles south of the town of Newcomb is an easy 3.8 mile round trip to the restored 60 foot fire tower. Views to the north of Rich Lake, Seward Range, Santanoni Range, and the Algonquin Range.

Lake George Region

Father Isaac Joques, a French Jesuit missionary, discovered Lake George in 1646. Over 100 years later General William Johnson renamed it Lake George. The lake is thirty two miles long and one to three miles wide. Sandy beaches, huge cliffs and mountains, many marshes and hundreds of islands make this region a favorite spot for recreation activities.

Brant Lake

Black Mountain

- Over fifty trails exist within the Lake George region. The highest peak at 2646 feet is Black Mountain. A moderate hike of eight miles round trip will take about six hours. One climbs vertically over 1100 feet. The open rock summit overlooks Lake George and its islands, the Adirondack High Peaks, the Hudson Valley, Lake Champlain, and Vermont.

Top Of The World

- A short drive south of Lake George is Top of the World with its beautiful vistas of Lake George. Black Mountain, on the eastern shore, is shrouded in a parade of clouds marching north over the lake.

Pharaoh Mountain Wilderness

- A vast wilderness area with numerous scenic vistas. A round trip of over 9 miles of hiking becomes progressively steeper as one climbs to the summit at 2557 feet. Crane Pond can be seen in the valley below.

Pharaoh Mountain Trail

- Crane Pond Road, a 2 mile one lane unimproved road, passes Alder Pond before starting up Pharaoh Mountain. For the first mile the trail is almost flat meandering through the forest.

Indian Lake And Blue Mountain Lake Region

Indian Lake

Lakes dominate the southern Adirondacks. Many of the largest lakes are on fault zones that were dammed up by glacial debris thousands of year ago. Indian Lake, Long Lake, Blue Mountain Lake, and Lake George are some of the more prominent lakes.

Indian Lake

- Here is Indian Lake where we camped to obtain this photograph at sunrise.

Blue Mountain Lake

- Over 60 miles of trail exist in this area. Blue Mountain trail is the most popular.

Lake Durant

- This lake was named after William West Durant in 1938, two years after his death, for his major contributions to the central Adirondack region. He conceived nineteenth century tourism in the central Adirondacks. Mr. Durant opened up the Raquette Lake region by building railroads, steamboats, a stagecoach line, and even telegraph lines. The lake is 327 acres and is located on the Northville Placid trail which affords many hiking opportunities.

Buttermilk Waterfall

- Between the towns of Long Lake and Blue Mountain is this beautiful waterfall.

Lake Pleasant

- Near the town of Speculator, thick fog rises from the cold waters of Lake Pleasant in early fall.

Tupper Lake Region

Piercefield Flow Near Tupper Lake

Around 1900 a man named Tupper surveyed the land around the lake that now bears his name. Logging and railroad individuals cleared the land around Tupper Lake thus connecting New York and Montreal. Rivers and lakes surround Tupper Lake making it a wilderness paradise.

Piercefield flow

- Within moments the sky and water changed from yellow to silver.

Wetlands

- This wetland area is between Tupper and Saranac Lake.

Dead Creek Flow

- This 2 mile plus trail around Dead Creek Flow leads to Cat Mountain and High Falls.

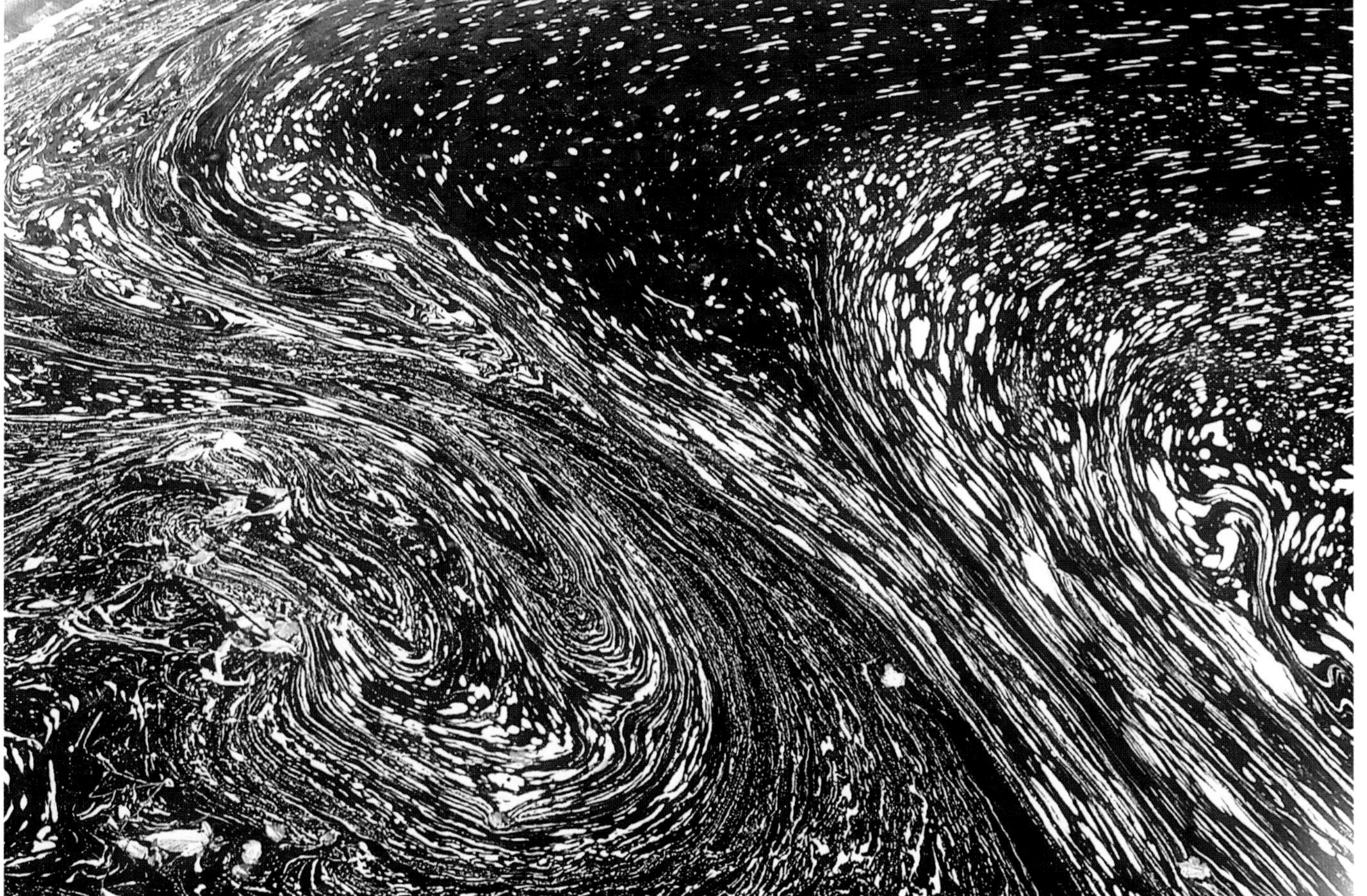

High Falls

- The hike to Cat Mountain and then on to High Falls is over 14 miles for the round trip. I did the hike in one day since the ground covered is flat although very wet in spots.

Dead Creek Flow

Raquette River Area

- A 5 mile trail follows many horse paths until it reaches the Raquette River itself. Unique rock formations dot the shoreline.

Raquette River

Paul Smiths Region

Paul Smiths Visitor Interpretive Center

Miles of paths await a leisurely walk along bark strewn paths at the Paul Smiths Visitor Interpretive Center. Near the waters edge bridges have been built to give you views of the wet lands in their fall beauty.

Geese

- Thousands of geese migrate through New York State each year with some stopping on their long journey in early spring to have their young. Three goslings can be seen here. One braving the cold temperatures and the other two barely visible under the warm feathers of the mother.

Paul Smiths Visitor Interpretive Center

- Five hiking trails exist within the center. Heron Marsh Trail, Barnum Brook Trail, Forest Ecology Trail, Shingle Mill Falls Trail, and Silverculture Trail. The shortest trail is .6 of a mile and the longest is 1.2 miles. Most are very easy to negotiate. Guided tours, self guided brochures, and scheduled classes are available. The views above are from Shingle Mill Falls Trail on the 300 foot long pontoon bridge.

Paul Smiths Visitor Interpretive Center

- Heron Marsh Trail is less than one mile with boardwalks that lead directly to the marsh areas. Observation towers and boardwalks along the route allow for a unique perspective of the area. Elaine Linnehan relaxes on one of the many benches provided for quiet observations of the wildlife.

Sunset near Harrietstown

- On Route 86, just past the junction of Route 186 to Lake Clear, puffy cumulous clouds parade across the fields of wheat. The setting sun illuminated the hills in the foreground while the mountains in the distance turn black.

Adirondack Sunrise

- Clouds swirl across the Adirondack mountains at sunrise.

Meacham Lake

- One can camp and hike at Meacham Lake State campgrounds. Until 1921 the Meacham Lake Hotel was located near the lake. New York State purchased the land in 1932 and constructed 224 camp sites. The campground is now the only development on the lake. The 1200 acre lake is surrounded by state forest land. Many trails exist in this wilderness area. On a cold clear autumn day, mist streams across the face of Debar Mountain.

Meacham Lake Outlet

- Just south of the main lake is the Meacham Lake outlet.

Barnum Pond

- Driving north on Route 30, just past Paul Smiths College and before Meacham Lake, is Barnum Pond. I arrived less than half an hour before sunrise. For less than twenty seconds the sun lit up the pond and these hills on the next page.

Barnum Pond

**There is a solitude, a satisfaction of being one with nature.
Of gathering strength from its strength.
In the fall, in the mist, in the reflections.
A wanting to preserve this feeling for generations to come.
From its magnificent mountain scenery to its great camps,
I hope this inspires you to join in the Adirondack's continued preservation.**

Alphabetized listing of photographs A through K

Alphabetized listing of photographs L through Z

Sunrise on Mt. Jo and the Algonquin range.

Purchase Photographs From Adirondack Splendor

Linnehan Press
6833 West Gulick Road
Naples, New York 14512
denlinn@sprynet.com

You may purchase selected photographs throughout the book:
Limited edition signed and numbered prints (1 to 50). E-mail or write for prices.